# WHAT OTHERS ARE SAYING ABOUT JIM ROHN...

*"Jim Rohn is one of the most articulate, powerful, thought provoking speakers I've seen. His unique delivery and style put him head and shoulders above the rest."*

**Harvey Mackay,**
**Author, "Swim with the Sharks**
**Without Being Eaten Alive"**

*"I don't believe there is another speaker in America today who can state the truth as vividly as Jim Rohn. His books and tapes have sustained us, but his seminars have empowered us."*

**Harlan Ritter,**
**CEO of Houston Belt and Terminal Railway**

*"Jim Rohn is a modern day Will Rogers. His perceptions of achievement and success have launched thousands of people on a wonderful, life-changing voyage into success and happiness. I can't recommend too strongly that you experience Jim Rohn personally."*

**Tom Hopkins,**
**President of Tom Hopkins International**

*"Jim Rohn is the most effective communicator of successful leadership and business principles of our time. He moves people to act!"*

**Rod Troutman,**
**Director of Sales & Training, United Consumers Club**

*"Mesmerizing! I've heard Jim Rohn speak on numerous occasions and I still listen intently to every word he says. His delivery is flawless; his ideas timeless."*

**Dr. Tony Alessandra,**
**Alessandra and Associates**

*"Some speakers have a great message to share, some speakers have a great delivery. Jim Rohn is one of the few speakers that has both. I believe Jim Rohn will become known as the best of the best."*

**George T. Jochum,**
**Chairman of the Board/CEO/President,**
**Mid Atlantic Medical Services, Inc.**

*"Jim Rohn is a world-class wordsmith who delivers clarity and meaning with his memorable mental meals."*

**Gerhard Gschwandtner, Publisher**
**quote from "Personal Selling Power"**

*"Jim Rohn's message is timeless and powerful. He is the Master Communicator. His insights are impactful and keep you on the edge of your chair wanting more."*

**Gordon Andrews,**
**Director, Center for Advanced Training**

*"Jim Rohn is outstanding! He is among the most polished, professional speakers in America, with a message everyone should hear."*

**Brian Tracy,**
**President of Brian Tracy Learning Systems**

*"Jim Rohn is one of the most articulate and compelling speakers of our time. His ideas and insights inspire people to test the limits of their potential."*

**Dr. Walter Doyle Staples,
Author, "Think Like A Winner!"**

*"From the first time I heard a Jim Rohn tape I was hooked! He paints a picture of success for people that everyone can star in. With his warm and engaging words, he lures you to profound wisdom that must be acted on by anyone seeking personal growth. He is one of those people you wish you were related to."*

**Séan D. McCardle
President, Life Answers**

*"Jim Rohn is the ultimate teacher, leader and speaker with a message that propels people to new levels of achievement and satisfaction."*

**Sandy Villas,
Co-author, "Power Networking"**

*"Having sent over 80 people to your one day seminar, and received their feedback, I have to conclude it was the best day in 13 years of sales and management training I have ever experienced."*

**Mike Wooten,
Senior Vice President, Primerica**

*"Jim Rohn, my first personal development teacher, always taught me that if you have enough reasons, you can do anything. Reasons are the difference between being interested versus being committed to accomplish something."*

**Anthony Robbins,**
**from his book, "Unlimited Power"**

*"Managers do things right. Leaders do the right things. Seven years ago, Jim Rohn taught me that difference, and it's made all the difference."*

**Karuna Kanagaratoran,**
**Founder and CEO of The Missing Piece**

*"Too often well known motivational speakers are best described as 'powerful,' 'dynamic,' 'humorous,' or even 'spellbinding.' Jim Rohn, although all of those, can best be described as 'impactful.'"*

**David Chilton**
**Author of "The Wealthy Barber"**

*"Jim Rohn helped me in risk taking and stretching in both my personal and professional life over the last 20 years. Jim is an insightful change-maker."*

**Danielle Kennedy,**
**Danielle Kennedy Productions**

# THE
# TREASURY
# OF
# QUOTES

## by

# JIM ROHN
### America's Foremost
### Business Philosopher

*"The Treasury of Quotes" by Jim Rohn is a collection of over 365 quotes gathered from Jim Rohn's personal journals, seminars, and books. These quotes reflect over 30 years of experience in business and in sharing ideas that affect people's lives.*

*To date, Jim Rohn's message has reached an audience of over 3 million people. May Jim's words now affect you, your family, friends, and business associates as you feast upon this treasury of life-changing ideas and inspiration.*

For more information about Jim Rohn, contact:

Jim Rohn International
9810 N. MacArthur
Suite 303
Irving, TX 75063
(214) 401-1000

Publisher:  Health Communications, Inc.
            3201 S.W. 15th Street
            Deerfield Beach, Florida 33442-8190

# DEDICATION

*To all those who have encouraged me to share my message with them over the past 30 years. This is for you!*

*Jim Rohn*

# ACKNOWLEDGEMENTS

This book covers three decades of the gathering of ideas that represent my current personal philosophy.

Giving full and proper recognition to all those whose lives, thoughts and words have affected my own is difficult, but a handful of individuals so deeply touched me that I must acknowledge their contribution as friends, as business associates, or as individuals.

My first and foremost recognition must be given to my mother and my father, who are the rock of my heritage.

To Mr. J. Earl Shoaff, who first introduced me to the uncommon thought that I could be more than I was, I will always be grateful.

To the men and women who have influenced my thinking, whose own words stimulated my imagination, and who on some occasions, shared the platform with me as together we sought to influence the lives of others. Among those are the late Earl Nightingale, Dr. Dennis Waitley, Zig Ziglar, Brian Tracy, Dr. Robert Schuller, the late Dr. Norman Vincent Peale, Tom Hopkins, Anthony Robbins, Danielle Kennedy, Tony Alessandra, and also those whose written words revealed a new world of possibilities, especially the fundamental truths found in the Bible.

With any good enterprise, one needs good people. To Kyle and Heide Wilson, who promoted me for five years before Heide went on to motherhood, leaving Kyle to assume full responsibility for the daily operations of Jim Rohn International. To Jerry Haines, Brian Dodge, Ron Marks, Terry Butler, and James and Wendy Rowan, long time promoters who still represent me through public seminars in the U.S. and overseas, as well as more recent promoters: Duncan McPherson, Dan Brattland, Mac Chapman, Ray Last, Jeff Howard, Michael Jeffries, Marian Wilson, and Karuna Kanagaratoran, I want to express my sincere thanks and encouragement. Let's be the best!

I am grateful to all my friends at Nightingale-Conant Corporation, including Vic Conant, Kevin McEneeley, Mike Willbond, and Robert Stuberg, who have helped in the production and distribution of many of my audio cassette programs.

Also, my sincere appreciation to Ron Reynolds and Kathryn Chinell, who have played a valuable role in product research and development.

And of course, to my two daughters and their families, who give me continuing reasons to pursue what I most believe in, and whose inspiration and encouragement keep me searching for new ways to express old truths.

*Jim Rohn*

# FOREWORD

When I was asked by WRS Publishing Group to write *The Greatest Speakers I Have Ever Heard,* Jim Rohn was the first speaker who came into my mind. Not only has his message meant a great deal in my life and business career, but literally thousands of the speakers I know through our Walters International Speakers Bureau have shared with me the same story of his inspiration.

As I wrote my book, I asked each of the speakers to tell me which great speaker had ignited the spark of creativity and achievement in their lives. Many told me, "Dottie, it was Jim Rohn."

The first time I heard Jim speak, I was in the midst of building an advertising business in order to help my husband. We were about to lose our tract home and a small dry cleaning business, in a recession period. I had the idea of writing an advertising column as I had done in high school. I started on foot, pushing my two babies ahead of me in a rickety old stroller with a wheel that came off frequently. The rural roads of Baldwin Park, California, a chicken ranching town, had no sidewalks.

Walking with my babies was hard, but even harder were the remarks by family, neighbors and friends who said, "Who do you think you are? You can't do that, you have no college education!"

Then a friend of mine invited me to go with her to hear Jim Rohn. We were seated at tables of 10 people. Next to me sat a middle-aged woman who seemed agitated at the behavior of her rebellious teenage son. If you have teenagers in your life, you understand how one can behave when you make him go where he does not want to go.

The boy was scrounched down so that his neck touched the back of the chair. His long legs, crossed at the ankle, were stretched out so that no one could pass our table without stepping over him or tripping. He folded his arms across his chest and stuck out his lower lip belligerently.

Then Jim Rohn began to speak. Jim has a soft, humorous, pleasant but powerful style, filled with many unforgettable stories. He told us tales of simple things like ants, and how they never give up.

Jim explained that you must act first. That God says to us, "If you don't move, I don't move." He said, "If you sow, you can reap - but you must sow first." And "Unless you change what you are, you will always have what you've got!"

His words clicked off the noise of my naysayers whose "ghetto blaster" remarks had been like rocks in my shoes. Jim let me see that it didn't matter what they said because only I know who I am and what I am capable of. I have read 6 books, mainly biographies, every week since I was a child. Jim said, "All the successful movers and shakers with whom I have had contact are good readers. All leaders are readers."

The boy quickly asked his mother for a
pen and paper. Then he leaned on the
table and began taking notes as fast as he
could write. He never stopped during the
entire program. The magic moment of
recognition had occurred. The boy caught
the bright light of Jim Rohn's ideas. He
realized they were true, because he already
knew them with his own heart and mind,
and he saw by their light who he was.

I have long wished for a book of Jim
Rohn's quotes. What a golden, glowing
treasure this book is. I warn you, it will
open up the doors of achievement for you
that you may have thought were nailed
shut. Turn the page. Jim has the lights
turned on for you.

*Dottie Walters*
*President, Walters International Speakers Bureau*
*Author, "The Greatest Speakers I Have Ever Heard"*

# TABLE OF CONTENTS

*SPECIAL EXCERPTS SECTION*

# INTRODUCTION

Words enable us to transfer our thoughts from inside our own mind into the mind of another. They have the power to alter history, to describe the past, and to bring meaning and substance to the present.

Words in the mind are like colors on the palette of the artist. The more colors we have access to, the easier it is to create a captivating picture on the canvass, and the more practice we give to using those many colors appropriately and uniquely, the more likely we will be to create a masterpiece of self-expression.

It has been said that Winston Churchill "organized the English language and sent it into battle." It was his unique choice of words and the intensity behind them that fueled the mind, rekindled the shaken spirit, and brought a new determination to the people of Great Britain in their time of great crisis. Without the powerful eloquence of this extraordinary man, the course of history may have made the present very different for us all.

There are many reasons why self-expression is such an important skill to master. Ultimately, the very quality of our own lives is largely determined by our ability to persuade and to convince others, as well as by our ability to transfer accurately our own thoughts and feelings into the mind of someone else.

Effective communication is a significant challenge. It cannot be mastered by a casual approach. Instead, we must take advantage of every opportunity life affords us to practice our ability to affect other people.

After three decades of sharing ideas with others, I am still astounded by the remarkable power of well-spoken words. My own life was completely transformed because of the inspiring and encouraging words of one man who saw in me more than I was then able to see in myself. That, in the final analysis, is the greatest contribution we can make to the life of another - to enable them to feel new hope, sense new emotions, and see new possibilities.

This book is a compilation of some of the thoughts I have written or spoken over the years. But I can take little credit for the originality of any of these expressions. Whatever understanding I may have of life and business is the result of having feasted on a rich diet of ideas from others whose words caused me to find new ways of expressing old ideas.

It is my hope that in these pages you will find the words that will stimulate you to stand up and step forth. After all, it was three simple words, spoken by a dying mother to her son, that dramatically changed the life of a boy and our nation. The words "Be somebody, Abe" so inspired a young boy from Illinois that he went on to become the sixteenth President of the United States.

I wish for you a similar journey, from where you may be at the moment, to where you want to go and to what you want to become.

May you live a remarkable and memorable life.

*Jim Rohn*

# THE
# TREASURY
## OF
# QUOTES

## by

# JIM ROHN
**America's Foremost
Business Philosopher**

# ACTIVITY/LABOR

*You must learn to translate wisdom and strong feelings into labor.*

*The miracle of the seed and the soil is not available by affirmation; it is only available by labor.*

*Make rest a necessity, not an objective. Only rest long enough to gather strength.*

*Without constant activity, the threats of life will soon overwhelm the values.*

*The few who do are the envy of the many who only watch.*

*For every promise, there is a price to pay.*

# AMERICA

*The Pledge of Allegiance starts with "I" and ends with "all." That's what America is all about - "I" (individual) and "all" (all of us). When all of us understand how valuable each of us is, that's powerful. And here's what else is powerful: When each of us understands how powerful all of us are.*

*America is unique because it offers you an economic ladder to climb. And here's what's exciting: It is the bottom of the ladder that is crowded, not the top.*

*In America we have the greatest chance for opportunity than anyone else in the past six and a half thousand years. Never in recorded history have so many different gifts been brought from all over the world and deposited in one country.*

*In America, everything you need to succeed is within reach.*

# ASKING/BELIEF/RESOLVE

*Asking is the beginning of receiving. Make sure you don't go to the ocean with a teaspoon. At least take a bucket so the kids won't laugh at you.*

*There is no better opportunity to receive more than to be thankful for what you already have. Thanksgiving opens the windows of opportunity for ideas to flow your way.*

*Resolve says, "I will." The man says, "I will climb this mountain. They told me it is too high, too far, too steep, too rocky, and too difficult. But it's my mountain. I will climb it. You will soon see me waving from the top or dead on the side from trying."*

*Disgust and resolve are two of the great emotions that lead to change.*

25

# BASICS/FUNDAMENTALS

*Success is neither magical nor mysterious. Success is the natural consequence of consistently applying basic fundamentals.*

*There are no new fundamentals. You've got to be a little suspicious of someone who says, "I've got a new fundamental." That's like someone inviting you to tour a factory where they are manufacturing antiques.*

*Some things you have to do every day. Eating seven apples on Saturday night instead of one a day just isn't going to get the job done.*

*Success is nothing more than a few simple disciplines, practiced every day; while failure is simply a few errors in judgement, repeated every day. It is the accumulative weight of our disciplines and our judgements that leads us to either fortune or failure.*

## BOOKS/LIBRARY/READING

*Most homes valued at over $250,000 have a library. That should tell us something.*

*Everything you need for your better future and success has already been written. And guess what? It's all available. All you have to do is go to the library. But would you believe that only three percent of the people in America have a library card. Wow, they must be expensive! No, they're free. And there's probably a library in every neighborhood. Only three percent!*

*Miss a meal if you have to, but don't miss a book.*

*Some people claim that it is okay to read trashy novels because sometimes you can find something valuable in them. You can also find a crust of bread in a garbage can, if you search long enough, but there is a better way.*

# BOOKS/LIBRARY/READING

*Some people read so little they have rickets of the mind.*

*It isn't what the book costs; it's what it will cost if you don't read it.*

*I now have one of the better libraries. I'll admit that I haven't read everything in my library, but I feel smarter just walking in it.*

*Books are easy to find and easy to buy. A paperback these days only costs six or seven dollars. You can borrow that from your kids!*

*Don't just read the easy stuff. You may be entertained by it, but you will never grow from it.*

*The book you don't read won't help.*

# CAREER/MARKETPLACE

*My father taught me to always do more than you get paid for as an investment in your future.*

*Whether you stay six weeks, six months, or six years, always leave it better than you found it.*

*Don't bring your need to the marketplace, bring your skill. If you don't feel well, tell your doctor, but not the marketplace. If you need money, go to the bank, but not the marketplace.*

*We get paid for bringing value to the marketplace. It takes time to bring value to the marketplace, but we get paid for the value, not for the time.*

*Here's the major problem with going on strike for more money: You cannot get rich by demand.*

# CAREER/MARKETPLACE

*If you make a sale, you can make a living. If you make an investment of time and good service in a customer, you can make a fortune.*

*Don't just let your business or your job make something for you; let it make something of you.*

*Lack of homework shows up in the marketplace as well as in the classroom*

*Where you start in the marketplace is not where you have to stay.*

*The worst days of those who enjoy what they do are better than the best days of those who don't.*

# CHANGE/CHOICE/DECISION

*I used to say, "I sure hope things will change." Then I learned that the only way things are going to change for me is when I change.*

*Don't say, "If I could, I would." Say, "If I can, I will."*

*It doesn't matter which side of the fence you get off on sometimes. What matters most is getting off! You cannot make progress without making decisions.*

*We generally change ourselves for one of two reasons: inspiration or desperation.*

*If you don't like how things are, change it! You're not a tree.*

31

# CHANGE/CHOICE/DECISION

*One of the best places to start to turn your life around is by doing whatever appears on your mental "I should" list.*

*Indecision is the thief of opportunity.*

*Every life form seems to strive to its maximum except human beings. How tall will a tree grow? As tall as it possibly can. Human beings, on the other hand, have been given the dignity of choice. You can choose to be all or you can choose to be less. Why not stretch up to the full measure of the challenge and see what all you can do?*

*You cannot change your destination overnight, but you can change your direction overnight.*

*Decision making can sometimes seem like inner civil war.*

# COMMUNICATION/PERSUASION

*The goal of effective communication should be for the listener to say, "Me, too!" versus "So what?"*

*Learn to express, not impress.*

*It's not the matter you cover so much as it is the manner in which you cover it.*

*Be brief on the logic and reason portion of your presentation. There are probably about a thousand facts about an automobile, but you don't need them all to make a decision. About a half dozen will do.*

*Better understated than overstated. Let people be surprised that it was more than you promised and easier than you said.*

# COMMUNICATION/PERSUASION

*For effective communication, use brevity. Jesus said, "Follow me." Now that's brief! He could be brief because of all that he was that he didn't have to say.*

*You cannot speak that which you do not know. You cannot share that which you do not feel. You cannot translate that which you do not have. And you cannot give that which you do not possess. To give it and to share it, and for it to be effective, you first need to have it. Good communication starts with good preparation.*

*Effective communication is 20% what you know and 80% how you feel about what you know.*

*What is powerful is when what you say is just the tip of the iceberg of what you know.*

34

# COMMUNICATION/PERSUASION

*If you just communicate, you can get by. But if you communicate skillfully, you can work miracles.*

*Don't mistake courtesy for consent.*

*It's so easy to make a mistake in language if you aren't careful. What if you meant to say, "What's troubling you?" and what you actually said was, "What's wrong with you?"*

*Real persuasion comes from putting more of you into everything you say. Words have an effect. Words loaded with emotion have a powerful effect.*

*Be careful of using inside lingo on the outside world.*

# COMMUNICATION/PERSUASION

*Take advantage of every opportunity to practice your communication skills so that when important occasions arise, you will have the gift, the style, the sharpness, the clarity, and the emotions to affect other people.*

*Communication is the ability to affect other people with words.*

*The more you know, the less you need to say.*

*Don't be afraid to borrow if someone else has said it well. Winston Churchill said, "The truth is incontrovertible. Malice may attack it and ignorance may deride it, but in the end, there it is." That's so well said. You could stay up all night and not think of that.*

# CONCENTRATION

*The best advice I ever came across on the subject of concentration is: Wherever you are, be there.*

*When you work, work. When you play, play. Don't mix the two.*

*Give whatever you are doing and whoever you are with the gift of your attention.*

*On the way to work, concentrate on the way - not on the work..*

*Pay attention. Don't just stagger through the day.*

37

# DEBATE

*Debate refines a good idea. That's why we have two major parties in Congress. Somebody says, "I have a great idea for the country." We say, "Wonderful! Put it on the table. Let's debate." And we start the debate by questioning the guy who has this great idea. After the third question he says, "I withdraw my great idea. I forgot about those three questions."*

*There is plenty of time to argue with new ideas later. The key is to take careful notes first and debate second.*

*Always be willing to look at both sides of the argument. Understanding the other side is the best way to strengthen your own.*

*We need to teach our children how to debate the major life issues. Debate strengthens their beliefs and enables them to defend themselves against ideologies that are going to come their way.*

# DESIRE/MOTIVATION

*Humans have the remarkable ability to get exactly what they must have. But there is a difference between a "must" and a "want."*

*The best motivation is self-motivation. The guy says, "I wish someone would come by and turn me on." What if they don't show up? You've got to have a better plan for your life..*

*When you know what you want, and you want it bad enough, you will find a way to get it.*

*Motivation alone is not enough. If you have an idiot and you motivate him, now you have a motivated idiot.*

*Without a sense of urgency, desire loses its value.*

39

# DISCIPLINE

*Discipline is the bridge between goals and accomplishment.*

*We must all suffer from one of two pains: the pain of discipline or the pain of regret. The difference is discipline weighs ounces while regret weighs tons.*

*One discipline always leads to another discipline.*

*Affirmation without discipline is the beginning of delusion.*

*You don't have to change that much for it to make a great deal of difference. A few simple disciplines can have a major impact on how your life works out in the next 90 days, let alone in the next 12 months or the next 3 years.*

40

# DISCIPLINE

*The least lack of discipline starts to erode our self-esteem.*

*All disciplines affect each other. Mistakenly the man says, "This is the only area where I let down." Not true. Every let down affects the rest. Not to think so is naive.*

*Discipline is the foundation upon which all success is built. Lack of discipline inevitably leads to failure.*

*Discipline has within it the potential for creating future miracles.*

*The best time to set up a new discipline is when the idea is strong.*

41

# EDUCATION/LEARNING

*Formal education will make you a living; self-education will make you a fortune.*

*We must learn to apply all that we know so that we can attract all that we want.*

*Learning is the beginning of wealth. Learning is the beginning of health. Learning is the beginning of spirituality. Searching and learning is where the miracle process all begins.*

*If someone is going down the wrong road, he doesn't need motivation to speed him up. What he needs is education to turn him around.*

*Don't see the mind for more than it is, but don't misread it for all that it can be.*

42

# EDUCATION/LEARNING

*Sharpen your interest in two major subjects: life and people. You will only gather information from a source if you are interested in it.*

*Education must precede motivation.*

*While you are in school, make sure you get the information. What you think about it, that's up to you. What you are going to do with it, that will soon be up to you. But while you are there, make sure you get it. In fact, my advice is - Don't leave school without it!*

*Never begrudge the money you spend on your own education.*

*If you step up the self-education curve, you will come up with more answers than you can use.*

# EMOTIONS

*Emotions will either serve or master, depending on who is in charge.*

*Our emotions need to be as educated as our intellect. It is important to know how to feel, how to respond, and how to let life in so that it can touch you.*

*Civilization is the intelligent management of human emotions.*

*Measure your emotions. You don't need an atomic explosion for a minor point.*

*Women have an incredible ability to pick up on emotional signals. For example, there are some wolves that are so clever they have learned to dress up like sheep. Man says, "Looks like a sheep. Talks like a sheep." Woman says, "Ain't no sheep!"*

# EMPATHY/CARING

*Show your contempt for the problem and your concern for the person.*

*Be sensitive to the plight of others. You have to know about the tragedies as well as the triumphs, the failures as well as the successes.*

*How do you build a bridge between age 12 and age 40? By remembering.*

*One of the greatest gifts you can give to anyone is the gift of your attention.*

*The more you care, the stronger you can be.*

*Don't operate on the heart with a hatchet.*

45

# ENTERPRISE

*Enterprise is better than ease.*

*Profits are better than wages. Wages make you a living; profits make you a fortune.*

*Human beings have the remarkable ability to turn nothing into something. They can turn weeds into gardens and pennies into fortunes.*

*Showing a profit means touching something and leaving it better than you found it.*

*Enterprise is the hope of our future.*

# EXPERIENCE

*Take time to gather up the past so that you will be able to draw from your experiences and invest them in the future.*

*Don't let the learning from your own experiences take too long. If you have been doing it wrong for the last ten years, I would suggest that's long enough!*

*Life is not just the passing of time. Life is the collection of experiences and their intensity.*

*It's easy to carry the past as a burden instead of a school. It's easy to let it overwhelm you instead of educate you.*

*Be like a sponge when it comes to each new experience. If you want to be able to express it well, you must first be able to absorb it well.*

# FAILURE

*The formula for disaster is: Could + Should + Won't.*

*Failure is not a single, cataclysmic event. You don't fail overnight. Instead, failure is a few errors in judgement, repeated every day.*

*Don't take the casual approach to life. Casualness leads to casualties.*

*It's too bad failures don't give seminars. Wouldn't that be valuable? If you meet a guy who has messed up his life for forty years, you've just got to say, "John, if I bring my journal and promise to take good notes, would you spend a day with me?"*

*Inevitability is being 200 feet from Niagara Falls in a little boat with no motor and no oars.*

# FASCINATION

*Fascination is one step beyond interest. Interested people want to know if it works. Fascinated people want to learn how it works.*

*Learn how to turn frustration into fascination. You will learn more being fascinated by life than you will by being frustrated by it.*

*I'm on my way to the airport to catch a plan that leaves in 45 minutes. The traffic is not moving one inch. I am now fascinated - not frustrated, but fascinated. But I must admit, it doesn't work every time.*

*Develop a childlike fascination with life and people.*

# FEAR/DOUBT/NEGATIVITY

*We must all wage an intense, lifelong battle against the constant downward pull. If we relax, the bugs and the weeds of negativity will move into the garden and take away everything of value.*

*Humility is a virtue; timidity is a disease.*

*If you spend five minutes complaining, you have just wasted five minutes. If you continue complaining, it won't be long before they haul you out to a financial desert and there let you choke on the dust of your own regret.*

*You cannot take the mild approach to the weeds in your garden. You've got to hate weeds enough to kill them. Weeds are not something you handle; weeds are something you devastate.*

# FINANCES/WEALTH

*The philosophy of the rich versus the poor is this: The rich invest their money and spend what is left; the poor spend their money and invest what is left.*

*I used to say, "Things cost too much." Then my teacher straightened me out on that by saying, "The problem isn't that things cost too much. The problem is that you can't afford it." That's when I finally understood that the problem wasn't "it" - the problem was "me!"*

*We all know a variety of ways to make a living. What's even more fascinating is figuring out ways to make a fortune.*

*The Bible says that it is hard for a rich man to enter into the kingdom of heaven. It doesn't say that it is impossible!*

51

# FINANCIAL INDEPENDENCE

*To become financially independent you must turn part of your income into capital; turn capital into enterprise; turn enterprise into profit; turn profit into investment; and turn investment into financial independence.*

*Part of your heritage in this society is the opportunity to become financially independent.*

*If you depend on your company to take care of your retirement, your future income will be divided by five. Take care of it yourself, and you can multiply your future income by five.*

*I remember saying to my mentor, "If I had more money, I would have a better plan." He quickly responded, "I would suggest that if you had a better plan, you would have more money." You see, it's not the amount that counts; it's the plan that counts.*

# FINANCIAL INDEPENDENCE

*If you were to show me your current financial plan, would I get so excited by it that I would go across the country and lecture on it? If the answer is no, then here's my question: Why not? Why wouldn't you have a superior financial plan that is taking you to the places you want to go?*

*Financial independence is the ability to live from the income of your own personal resources.*

*Shortly after I met my mentor he asked me," Mr. Rohn, how much money have you saved and invested over the last six years?" And I said, "None." He then asked, 'Who sold you on that plan?"*

*It is better to be a lender than a spender.*

# GIVING/SHARING/GENEROSITY

*It's best to start the discipline of generosity when the amounts are small. It's easy to give ten cents out of a dollar; it's a little harder to give a hundred thousand out of a million.*

*Giving is better than receiving because giving starts the receiving process.*

*Nothing teaches character better than generosity.*

*Here's what is exciting about sharing ideas with others: If you share a new idea with ten people, they get to hear it once and you get to hear it ten times.*

*Sharing makes you bigger than you are. The more you pour out, the more life will be able to pour in.*

# GIVING/SHARING/GENEROSITY

*Somebody says, "Well, I can't be concerned about other people. About the best I can do is to take care of myself." Well, then you will always be poor.*

*What you give becomes an investment that will return to you multiplied at some point in the future.*

*When somebody shares, everybody wins.*

*The amount you give isn't important. What matters is what that amounts represents in terms of your life.*

*Only by giving are you able to receive more than you already have.*

# GOALS/GOAL SETTING

*Goals. There's no telling what you can do when you get inspired by them. There's no telling what you can do when you believe in them. And there's no telling what will happen when you act upon them.*

*If you go to work on your goals, your goals will go to work on you. If you go to work on your plan, your plan will go to work on you. Whatever good things we build end up building us.*

*Don't set your goals too low. If you don't need much, you won't become much.*

*We all have two choices: We can make a living or we can design a life.*

*We all need lots of powerful long-range goals to help us past the short-term obstacles.*

# GOALS/GOAL SETTING

*The major reason for setting a goal is for what it makes of you to accomplish it. What it makes of you will always be the far greater value than what you get.*

*The ultimate reason for setting goals is to entice you to become the person it takes to achieve them.*

*When Andrew Carnegie died, they discovered a sheet of paper upon which he had written one of the major goals of his life: to spend the first half of his life accumulating money and to spend the last half of his life giving it all away.*

*Some people are disturbed by those tough days because all they have is the days. They haven't designed or described or defined the future.*

# GOVERNMENT

*It can be dangerous to weaken the strong in our attempts to strengthen the weak.*

*One of the great liberal documents of the world is the Declaration of Independence. One of the great conservative documents of the world is the Constitution of the United States. We need both documents to build a country. One to get it started - liberal. And the other to help maintain the structure over the years - conservative.*

*Beware of those who seek to take care of you lest your caretakers become your jailers.*

*Taxes are our way of feeding the goose that lays the golden eggs of freedom, democracy, and enterprise. Someone says, "Well, the goose eats too much." That's probably true. But better a fat goose than no goose at all!*

# GOVERNMENT

*Tyranny knows no restraint of appetite.*

*Did you ever eat a government cookie? The real genius to make a marketplace flourish does not come from the government, it comes from the genius of the people.*

*An ancient script asks, "Would you let a man rule the city who cannot even rule his own spirit?" Sometimes we do.*

*You cannot base your life on what the government does or how your tax dollars are being spent. You've got to vote well, and then chart your own course; vote well, and then take charge of your own life.*

*Sure the government has some pounds to lose, but don't we all? Let not one appetite accuse another.*

# HAPPINESS

*Learn how to be happy with what you have while you pursue all that you want.*

*Happiness is not an accident. Nor is it something you wish for. Happiness is something you design.*

*How sad to see a father with money and no joy. The man studied economics, but never studied happiness.*

*The greatest source of unhappiness comes from inside.*

*Happiness is the art of learning how to get joy from your substance.*

*Happiness is not something you postpone for the future; it is something you design for the present.*

# HEALTH

*Some people don't do well simply because they don't feel well.*

*Some people take better care of their pets than they do themselves. Their animals can run like the wind and they can barely make it up a flight of stairs.*

*Make sure the outside of you is a good reflection of the inside of you.*

*Treat your body like a temple, not a woodshed. The mind and the body work together. Your body needs to be a good support system for the mind and the spirit. If you take good care of it, your body can take you wherever you want to go, with the power and strength and energy and vitality you will need to get there.*

*Take good care of your body. It's the only place you have to live.*

# IDEAS

*If you wish to find, you must search. Rarely does a good idea interrupt you.*

*Ideas can be life-changing. Sometimes all you need to open the door is just one more good idea.*

*Ideas are information taking shape.*

*When a new idea comes our way, we must put it on our mental scales and weigh it carefully before deciding its value.*

*One of the secrets to success is ideas mixed with inspiration.*

*Nothing is more powerful for your future than being a gatherer of good ideas and information. That's called doing your homework.*

# IGNORANCE

*Ignorance is **not** bliss. Ignorance is poverty. Ignorance is devastation. Ignorance is tragedy. And ignorance is illness. It all stems from ignorance.*

*What you don't know **will** hurt you.*

*The worst kind of arrogance is arrogance from ignorance.*

*There is an ancient script that says, "He that wishes to be ignorant, let him be ignorant." But I took off the last word and it now reads for me like this: He that wishes to be ignorant, let him be!*

# INFLUENCE/ASSOCIATION

*There are two parts to influence: First, influence is powerful; and second, influence is subtle. You wouldn't let someone push you off course, but you might let someone nudge you off course and not even realize it.*

*We need a variety of input and influence and voices. You cannot get all the answers to life and business from one person or from one source.*

*Attitude is greatly shaped by influence and association.*

*Don't spend most of your time on the voices that don't count. Tune out the shallow voices so you will have more time to tune in the valuable ones.*

*"No" puts distance between you and the wrong influences.*

# INFLUENCE/ASSOCIATION

*You must constantly ask yourself these questions: Who am I around? What are they doing to me? What have they got me reading? What have they got me saying? Where do they have me going? What do they have me thinking? And most important, what do they have me becoming? Then ask yourself the big question: Is that okay?*

*Don't join an easy crowd; you won't grow. Go where the expectations and the demands to perform are high.*

*Some people you can afford to spend a few minutes with, but not a few hours.*

*Get around people who have something of value to share with you. Their impact will continue to have a significant effect on your life long after they have departed.*

# JOURNALS

*Be a collector of good ideas, but don't trust your memory. The best collecting place for all of the ideas and information that comes your way is your journal.*

*The reason why I spend so much money for my journals is to press me to find something valuable to put in them.*

*There are three things to leave behind: your photographs, your library, and your personal journals. These things are certainly going to be more valuable to future generations than your furniture!*

*Don't use your mind for a filing cabinet. Use your mind to work out problems and find answers; file away good ideas in your journal.*

# KIDS

*Kids are curious. Kids are watching ants while adults are stepping on them.*

*How many languages can a child learn? As many as you will take the time to teach them.*

*Even kids can get started on becoming financially independent. Kids can make profits long before they can legitimately earn wages.*

*Of course, kids should pay taxes. Tell little Johnny that if he wants to ride his bicycle on the sidewalk instead of in the mud, he's got to pay three more pennies when he buys a candy bar.*

*Kids ought to have two bicycles: one to ride and one to rent.*

# KIDS

*Kids don't lack capacity, only teachers.*

*I teach kids how to be rich by the time they are age 40; 35 if they are extra bright. Most kids think they are extra bright, so they go for the 35.*

*What should a child do with a dollar? Here's one philosophy: It's only a child and it's only a dollar, so what difference does it make? Wow, what a philosophy! Where do you suppose everything starts for the future? Here's where it starts - it starts with a child and a dollar. You say, "Well, he's only a child once. Let him spend it all." Well, when would you hope that would stop? When he's fifty and broke like you?*

*If kids clearly see the promise, they will gladly pay the price.*

# LEADERSHIP/MANAGEMENT

*The challenge of leadership is to be strong, but not rude; be kind, but not weak; be bold, but not a bully; be thoughtful, but not lazy; be humble, but not timid; be proud, but not arrogant; have humor, but without folly.*

*We must learn to help those who deserve it, not just those who need it. Life responds to deserve, not need.*

*My mentor said, "Let's go do it," not "You go do it." How powerful when someone says, "Let's!"*

*Good people are found, not changed. Recently, I read a headline that said, "We don't teach our people to be nice. We simply hire nice people." Wow! What a clever short cut.*

# LEADERSHIP/MANAGEMENT

*A good objective of leadership is to help those who are doing poorly to do well and to help those who are doing well to do even better.*

*If you share a good idea long enough, it will eventually fall on good people.*

*Leadership is the challenge to be something more than average.*

*Leaders, whether in the family, in business, in government, or in education, must not allow themselves to mistake intentions for accomplishments.*

*Learn to help people with more than just their jobs; help them with their lives.*

# LEADERSHIP/MANAGEMENT

*Sometimes those who need it the most are inclined the least.*

*In leadership we teach: Don't send your ducks to eagle school because it won't help. Duck finishes eagle school, sees his first rabbit, makes him a friend.*

*Start with where people are before you try to take them to where you want them to go.*

*Leaders must understand that some people will inevitably sell out to the evil side. Don't waste your time wondering why; spend your time discovering who.*

*Lead the way by personal example and by personal philosophy.*

# LEADERSHIP/MANAGEMENT

*Leaders must not be naive. I used to say, "Liars shouldn't lie." What a sad waste of words that is! I found out liars are supposed to lie. That's why we call them liars - they lie! What else would you expect them to do?*

*Managers help people to see themselves as they are. Leaders help people to see themselves better than they are.*

*When dealing with people, I generally take the obvious approach. When someone says, "This always happens to me and that always happens to me. Why do these things always happen to me?" I simply say, "Beats me. I don't know. All I know is that those kinds of things seem to happen to people like you."*

*We could all use a little coaching. When you're playing the game, it's hard to think of everything.*

# LIFESTYLE

*Lifestyle is the art of discovering ways to live uniquely.*

*Let others lead small lives, but not you. Let others argue over small things, but not you. Let others cry over small hurts, but not you. Let others leave their future in someone else's hands, but not you.*

*Some people have learned to earn well but they haven't learned to live well.*

*Lifestyle is not an amount; it's a practice.*

*Earn as much money as you possibly can and as quickly as you can. The sooner you get money out of the way, the sooner you will be able to get to the rest of your problems in style.*

# NEGLECT

*One of the reasons why many people don't have what they want is neglect.*

*We've all heard the expression, "An apple a day keeps the doctor away." Well, I've got a good question for you: What if it's true? Wouldn't that be easy to do - to eat an apple a day? Here's the problem: It's also easy not to do.*

*Neglect starts out as an infection then becomes a disease.*

*Cardiovascular problems alone in America create over a thousand funerals a day...and 90% of the problem is neglect.*

# PARENTING

*There is no greater leadership challenge than parenting.*

*If you talk to your children, you can help them to keep their lives together. If you talk to them skillfully, you can help them to build future dreams.*

*Leadership is the great challenge of the '90s in science, politics, education, and industry. But the greatest challenge in leadership is parenting. We need to do more than just get our enterprises ready for the challenges of the twenty-first century. We also need to get our children ready for the challenges of the twenty-first century.*

*Some people are careful with their customers and careless with their children.*

# PERSEVERANCE/PERSISTENCE

*It takes time to build a corporate work of art. It takes time to build a life. And it takes time to develop and grow. So give yourself, your enterprise, and your family the time they deserve and the time they require.*

*Americans are incredibly impatient. Someone once said that the shortest period of time in America is the time between when the light turns green and when you hear the first horn honk.*

*The twin killers of success are impatience and greed.*

*How long should you try? Until.*

*Some people plant in the spring and leave in the summer. If you've signed up for a season, see it through. You don't have to stay forever, but at least stay until you see it through.*

# PERSONAL DEVELOPMENT

*Income seldom exceeds personal development.*

*What you become directly influences what you get.*

*We can have more than we've got because we can become more than we are.*

*The big challenge is to become all that you have the possibility of becoming. You cannot believe what it does to the human spirit to maximize your human potential and stretch yourself to the limit.*

*Pity the man who inherits a million dollars and who isn't a millionaire. Here's what would be pitiful: If your income grew and you didn't.*

# PERSONAL DEVELOPMENT

*To attract attractive people, you must be attractive. To attract powerful people, you must be powerful. To attract committed people, you must be committed. Instead of going to work on them, you go to work on yourself. If you become, you can attract.*

*The most important question to ask on the job is not "What am I getting?" The most important question to ask on the job is "What am I becoming?"*

*It is hard to keep that which has not been obtained through personal development.*

*After you become a millionaire, you can give all of your money away because what's important is not the million dollars; what's important is the person you have become in the process of becoming a millionaire.*

78

# PERSONAL PHILOSOPHY

*The key factor that will determine your financial future is not the economy; the key factor is your philosophy.*

*Don't borrow someone else's plan. Develop your own philosophy and it will lead you to unique places.*

*If you learn to set a good sail, the wind that blows will always take you to the dreams you want, the income you want, and the treasures of mind, purse, and soul you want.*

*Your philosophy determines whether you will go for the disciplines or continue the errors.*

*Philosophy is the sum total of all that you know and what you decide is valuable.*

# PERSONAL PHILOSOPHY

*Economic disaster begins with a philosophy of doing less and wanting more.*

*If you want to amend your errors, you must begin by amending your philosophy.*

*The only thing worse than not reading a book in the last ninety days is not reading a book in the last ninety days and think that it doesn't matter.*

*Your personal philosophy is the greatest determining factor in how your life works out.*

*Initial response illustrates a great deal about someone's personal philosophy.*

*Only human beings can reorder their lives any day they choose by refining their philosophy.*

80

# PERSONAL RESPONSIBILITY

*Don't become a victim of yourself. Forget about the thief waiting in the alley; what about the thief in your mind?*

*It is not what happens that determines the major part of your future. What happens, happens to us all. It is what you do about what happens that counts.*

*You say, "The country is messed up." That's like cursing the soil and the seed and the sunshine and the rain, which is all you've got. Don't curse all you've got. When you get your own planet, you can rearrange this whole deal. This one you've got to take like it comes.*

*Walk away from the 97% crowd. Don't use their excuses. Take charge of your own life.*

81

# PERSONAL RESPONSIBILITY

*Take advice, but not orders. Only give yourself orders. Abraham Lincoln once said, "Since I will be no one's slave, I will be no one's master."*

*You must take personal responsibility. You cannot change the circumstances, the seasons, or the wind, but you can change yourself. That is something you have charge of. You don't have charge of the constellations, but you do have charge of whether you read, develop new skills, and take new classes.*

*Your paycheck is not your employer's responsibility, it's your responsibility. Your employer has no control over your value, but you do.*

*It is easier to blame the government than it is your own philosophy.*

82

# PLANNING

*I find it fascinating that most people plan their vacations with better care than they plan their lives. Perhaps that is because escape is easier than change.*

*If you don't design your own life plan, chances are you'll fall into someone else's plan. And guess what they may have planned for you? Not much.*

*The reason why most people face the future with apprehension instead of anticipation is because they don't have it well designed.*

*The guy says, "When you work where I work, by the time you get home, it's late. You've got to have a bite to eat, watch a little TV, relax, and get to bed. You can't sit up half the night planning, planning, planning." And he's the same guy who is behind on his car payment!*

83

# POSITIVE/NEGATIVE

*Learn from the negative as well as the positive, from the failures as well as the successes.*

*Life, in all its uniqueness, would not be life without the negatives and the positives. That is why it is important to be a serious student of both.*

*Life is part positive and part negative. Suppose you went to hear a symphony orchestra and all they played were little, happy, high notes? Would you leave soon? Let me hear the rumble of the bass, the crash of the cymbals, and the minor keys.*

*Life is a process of accumulation. We either accumulate the debt or the value, the regret or the equity.*

# PROBLEM SOLVING

*To solve any problem, here are three questions to ask yourself: First, what could I do? Second, what could I read? And third, who could I ask?*

*The real problem is usually two or three questions deep. If you want to go after someone's problem, be aware that most people aren't going to reveal what the real problem is after the first question.*

*Neil Armstrong once said, "You only have to solve two problems when going to the moon: first, how to get there; and second, how to get back. The key is don't leave until you have solved both problems."*

*Never attack a problem without also presenting a solution.*

*The best place to solve a problem is on paper.*

85

# RELATIONSHIPS

*One person caring about another represents life's greatest value.*

*Your family and your love must be cultivated like a garden. Time, effort, and imagination must be summoned constantly to keep any relationship flourishing and growing.*

*The greatest gift you can give to somebody is your own personal development. I used to say, "If you will take care of me, I will take care of you." Now I say, "I will take care of me for you if you will take care of you for me."*

*The walls we build around us to keep out the sadness also keep out the joy.*

*You cannot succeed by yourself. It's hard to find a rich hermit.*

# REPUTATION

*Each of us must be committed to maintaining the reputation of all of us. And all of us must be committed to maintaining the reputation of each of us.*

*Accuracy builds credibility.*

*It only takes one lie to taint your entire testimony.*

*The Bible gives us a list of human stories on both sides of the ledger. One list of human stories is used as examples - do what these people did. Another list of human stories is used as warnings - don't do what these people did. So if your story ever gets in one of these books, make sure they use it as an example, not a warning.*

# RESULTS

*At the end of each day, you should play back the tapes of your performance. The results should either applaud you or prod you.*

*The greatest form of maturity is at harvest time. That is when we must learn how to reap without complaint if the amounts are small and how to reap without apology if the amounts are big.*

*Life asks us to make measurable progress in reasonable time. That's why they make those fourth grade chairs so small - so you won't fit in them at age twenty-five!*

*There are some things you don't have to know how it works - only that it works. While some people are studying the roots, others are picking the fruit. It just depends which end of this you want to get in on.*

# SALES

*To succeed in sales, simply talk to lots of people every day. And here's what's exciting - there are lots of people!*

*Practice is just as valuable as a sale. The sale will make you a living; the skill will make you a fortune.*

*Sales is a person to person business. You cannot send the sales manual out to make the sale. Sales manuals have no legs and no voice.*

*In the sales profession the real work begins after the sale is made.*

*Sales people should take lessons from their kids. What does the word "no" mean to a child? Almost nothing!*

*Even if you are new in sales, you can make up in numbers what you lack in skills.*

89

# SERVICE

*One customer, well taken care of, could be more valuable than $10,000 worth of advertising.*

*Good service leads to multiple sales. If you take good care of your customers, they will open doors you could never open by yourself.*

*How do you deserve a fortune? Render fortunes of service.*

*You have to do more than you get paid for because that's where the fortune is.*

*Whoever renders service to many puts himself in line for greatness - great wealth, great return, great satisfaction, great reputation, and great joy.*

# SKILLS

*Don't wish it was easier; wish you were better. Don't wish for less problems; wish for more skills. Don't wish for less challenges; wish for more wisdom.*

*You must either modify your dreams or magnify your skills.*

*You can cut down a tree with a hammer, but it takes about 30 days. If you trade the hammer for an axe, you can cut it down in about 30 minutes. The difference between 30 days and 30 minutes is skill.*

*The key to life is to become skillful enough to be able to do rewarding things.*

*Learn to hide your need and show your skill.*

# SOPHISTICATION

Most people are just trying to get through the day. Sophisticated people learn how to get from the day.

Sophistication is understanding the difference between trinkets and treasures.

Don't spend major money on minor things. In the last ten years the guy has bought two tons of donuts and only two books - and the books are filled primarily with pictures.

Sophisticated people don't leave early. The man says, "Yeah, but I want to beat the traffic." Isn't that a great skill to have - beating the traffic!

It doesn't take a million dollars to learn the difference between a bottle of fine wine and a Pepsi. Sophistication is a study, not an amount.

# SOPHISTICATION

*One of the early signs of sophistication is not giving way to all inclinations but rather sending your emotions to school so they will learn how to behave.*

*Money doesn't make you sophisticated. Only study and practice make you sophisticated. Even people of modest means can become sophisticated because it is within study and practice. How much is a night out at the symphony? About thirty dollars. You say, "Poor people can't afford thirty dollars to go to the symphony." Yes, they can. It's only thirty Hershey bars!*

*We must teach our children not to spend their money a dollar at a time. If you spend your money a dollar at a time, you'll wind up with trinkets instead of treasures. You can't buy much of value a dollar at a time.*

# SOWING/REAPING

*You must get good at one of two things: sowing in the spring or begging in the fall.*

*God has the tough end of the deal. What if instead of planting the seed you had to make the tree? That would keep you up late at night, trying to figure that one out.*

*Plant, don't chant.*

*One of my good friends always says, "Things don't just happen; things happen just."*

*The soil says, "Don't bring me your need, bring me your seed."*

# STEWARDSHIP

*How much should you earn? As much as you possibly can. It doesn't matter whether you earn $10,000 a year or $1,000,000 a year as long as you've done the best you can.*

*The man says, "If I had a fortune, I'd take good care of it. But I only have a paycheck and I don't know where it all goes." Wouldn't you love to have him running your company?*

*If you wish to have power and influence over the many, be faithful (disciplined) when there is just a few. If you have a few employees, a few distributors, a few people, that's the time to stay in touch and be totally absorbed - when there is just a few.*

*Start from wherever you are and with whatever you've got.*

# STUDENT

*Be a student of the fine, not just the mundane and the ordinary that sustains our lives. We all need to be students of refinement, not just existence.*

*Always be eager to learn, no matter how successful you might already be. In the Millionaires' Club, we sometimes invite a billionaire to come talk to us. He says, "You're doing okay, but come on. How about if you really poured it on!"*

*Be a student, not a follower. Don't just go do what someone says. Take interest in what someone says, then debate it, ponder it, and consider it from all angles.*

*Don't read a book and be a follower; read a book and be a student.*

# SUCCESS

*Success is not to be pursued; it is to be attracted by the person you become.*

*Success is not so much what we have as it is what we are.*

*Success is 20% skills and 80% strategy.*

*Success lies in the opposite direction of the normal pull.*

*Success is the study of the obvious Everyone should take Obvious 1 and Obvious 2 in school.*

*Average people look for ways of getting away with it; successful people look for ways of getting on with it.*

# TIME MANAGEMENT

*Time is our most valuable asset, yet we tend to waste it, kill it, and spend it rather than invest it.*

*We can no more afford to spend major time on minor things than we can to spend minor time on major things.*

*Time is more valuable than money. You can get more money, but you cannot get more time.*

*Never begin the day until it is finished on paper.*

*Learn how to say no. Don't let your mouth overload your back.*

*Time is the best kept secret of the rich.*

# TIME MANAGEMENT

*Something will master and something will serve. Either you run the day or the day runs you; either you run the business or the business runs you.*

*Learn how to separate the majors and the minors. A lot of people don't do well simply because they major in minor things.*

*Don't mistake movement for achievement. It's easy to get faked out by being busy. The question is: Busy doing what?*

*Days are expensive. When you spend a day, you have one less day to spend. So make sure you spend each one wisely.*

*Sometimes you need to stay in touch but be out of reach.*

# TRUTH

*Very few of us are authorities on the truth. About the closest that any of us can get is what we hope is the truth or what we think is the truth. That's why the best approach to truth is probably to say, "It seems to me..."*

*There is nothing wrong with affirmations, provided what you are affirming is the truth. If you are broke, for example, the best thing to affirm is, "I'm broke!"*

*If the truth isn't enough, then you must become stronger at presenting it.*

*Sincerity is not a test of truth. We must not make this mistake: He must be right; he's so sincere. It is possible to be sincerely wrong. We can only judge truth by truth and sincerity by sincerity.*

*Find someone who is willing to share the truth with you.*

# VALUE

*Count the cost first. Don't pay too big a price for pursuing minor values.*

*The major value in life is not what you get. The major value in life is what you become. That is why I wish to pay fair price for every value. If I have to pay for it or earn it, that makes something of me. If I get it for free, that makes nothing of me.*

*All values must be won by contest, and after they have been won, they must be defended.*

*Don't sell out your virtue and your value for something you think you want. Judas got the money, but he threw it all away and hung himself because he was so unhappy with himself.*

*Values were meant to be costly. If it doesn't cost much, we probably wouldn't appreciate the value.*

# WORDS/VOCABULARY

*The two great words of antiquity are behold and beware.*

*Vocabulary enables us to interpret and to express. If you have a limited vocabulary, you will also have a limited vision and a limited future.*

*Well chosen words mixed with measured emotions is the basis of affecting people.*

*It's okay to send flowers, but don't let flowers do all the talking. Flowers have a limited vocabulary. About the best flowers can say is that you remembered.*

*Words do two major things: They provide food for the mind and create light for understanding and awareness.*

## ENLIGHTENED SELF-INTEREST
### (an excerpt from "The Weekend Seminar")

*Self-preservation has a tendency to lead to poverty. If you want to be the ruler over many, be faithful when there are just a few. A guy says, "Oh, if I had a big organization, then I'd really pour it on. But I just have a few and I don't know where they're at." If you just have a few distributors, a few employees, that's the time to sharpen your skills of communication and pour it on. When there are just a few, give it all you've got.*

*You must make the personal investment for the present to get ready for the future. The personal investment in education, personal investment in discipline, personal investment in discovery, personal investment in being a good parent. Do it in those early years so you can then put yourself in the position of being entrusted with larger treasures of fortune and people and equity.*

# GOOD AND EVIL
(an excerpt from "The Weekend Seminar")

*All leaders must understand the story of the frog and the scorpion. According to the story, the frog and the scorpion appeared on the bank of a river about the same time. The frog was about to jump into the river and swim to the other side. Along comes the scorpion who says to the frog, "Mr. Frog, I see that you are about to jump into the river and swim to the other side. Since I am a scorpion and cannot swim, would you let me hop on your back, and then you swim across the river and deposit me on the other side? I would be grateful."*

*The frog looked at the scorpion and said, "No way. You're a scorpion and scorpions sting frogs and kill them. I'd get half way with you on my back and you'd sting me and I'd die. You think I'm crazy? No way."*

*The scorpion said, "Hey, hold it a minute. With your frog brain, you're not thinking. If I were to sting you half way out there, sure you'd drown and die, but so would I since I'm a scorpion and cannot swim. That would be kind of foolish, so I'm not about to do that. I just want to get to the other side."*

*The frog considered the scorpion's reasoning and said, "That makes sense. Hop on." And according to the story, the scorpion hops onto the frog's back. They start across the river and, sure enough, half way across the river the scorpion stings the frog. They are now both about to go down for the third time. The frog cannot believe what has happened and he says to the scorpion, "Why did you do that? I'm about to die and drown, but so are you. Why did you do that?"*

*And the scorpion said, "Because I am a scorpion."*

*So all leaders must understand the story of the frog and the scorpion. There are shepherds and there are sheep and there are wolves. And wise leaders must understand that some wolves are so clever they've learned to dress up like sheep. But do not miss the story of the full drama of life called good and evil. It's part of the test of leadership skills.*

**105**

# SUCCESS IS EASY
(an excerpt from
"The Challenge to Succeed Seminar")

*People often ask me how I became successful in that six-year period of time while many of the people I knew did not. The answer is simple: The things I found to be easy to do, they found to be easy not to do. I found it easy to set the goals that could change my life. They found it easy not to. I found it easy to read the books that could affect my thinking and my ideas. They found that easy not to. I found it easy to attend the classes and the seminars, and to get around other successful people. They said it probably really wouldn't matter. If I had to sum it up, I would say what I found to be easy to do, they found to be easy not to do. Six years later, I'm a millionaire and they are all still blaming the economy, the government, and company policies, yet they neglected to do the basic, easy things.*

# MOTIVATION
### (an excerpt from
### "The Challenge to Succeed Seminar")

*Motivation is a mystery. Why does one salesperson see his first prospect at seven in the morning and another salesperson is just getting out of bed at eleven? I don't know. It's part of the mysteries of life. Give a lecture to a thousand people. One walks out and says, "I'm going to change my life." Another one walks out with a yawn, muttering to himself. "I've heard all this before." Why is that? Why wouldn't both be affected the same way? Another mystery. The millionaire says to a thousand people, "I read this book and it started me on the road to wealth." Guess how many go out and get the book? Very few. Isn't that incredible? Why wouldn't everyone get the book? A mystery of life. My suggestion would be to walk away from the 90% who don't and join the 10% who do.*

## LIFESTYLE
### (an excerpt from "The Art of Exceptional Living")

*It's really not hard to learn the art of living well. Even people with modest means can experience the sophisticated lifestyle. They simply save up some of their soda money for a bottle of fine wine. They skip going to the movies and attend the theater. By saving up their money all year, they have enough for a trip to Europe or a fine work of art.*

*Don't spend all of your money a quarter at a time. Save up and buy something special, something fine, something of lasting value, or something that will give you rich memories for a lifetime. Remember, all that candy money can add up to a small fortune. And for a sophisticated person, quality is far more important than quantity. Better a few treasures than a house full of junk.*

# ACTIVITY
### (an excerpt from
### "Take Charge of Your Life")

*Sometimes we don't ask for productivity right away. All we ask for at first is activity. Now, it's pretty easy to check activity. If someone joined the sales organization and he is supposed to make ten calls the first week, it's pretty simple on Friday to say, "John, how many calls did you make?" John says, "Well..." You say, "John, 'Well...' won't fit in my little box here." And John starts on a story. You say, "John, the reason why I made this box so small is so a story won't fit. I just need an activity number from one to ten."*

*If the results on activity after the first week are not good, that has to be a signal. You might try another week. Ultimately, you've got to be the judge about how far you will go in putting a team together with somebody's lack of precise activity.*

# PROBLEM SOLVING
### (an excerpt from
### "How To Use A Journal")

*One of the unique characteristics of a journal is that is offers you an effective way to figure it all out - to figure out life, to figure out people, to figure out business dilemmas, and most important of all, to figure out yourself.*

*There is something magical about putting a problem in writing. It is almost as though by writing about what is wrong, you start to discover new ways of making it right. Writing creates a space between you and the problem, and it is within this space that solutions have room to grow.*

*Writing about events and circumstances helps you to clarify exactly what is going on. When you describe a situation in writing, you tend to become more factual, more accurate, and certainly more realistic. Once you finally see things as they really are, you can then see your way clear to making them better.*

# FINANCIAL INDEPENDENCE FOR TEENAGERS
### (an excerpt from "The Three Keys to Greatness")

*If a child has a dollar, what should he do with it? How you answer this question is very important because it could determine what he does with his money for the rest of his life. You say, "Well, it's just a child and it's just a dollar." We call that massive errors in judgement.*

*If the child wants to spend the whole dollar, you have to say," No! You can't spend the whole dollar." The child asks why not? You say, "Let me show you why not." And take him to the other side of town and ask, "Would you like to live here? Here's where the people live who spend all they make." There's nothing better than a visual illustration to get the point across to a child. Show them the tragic circumstances if you spend all you've got. Kids will come home with big, wide eyes. Then ask, "Would you like to live like that?" Kid says, "No way!" And then you explain, "That's why you can't spend the whole dollar."*

111

# HOW WILL MY LIFE CHANGE?
### (an excerpt from
### "How To Have Your Best Year Ever")

*What's it going to be like in the year 2000? It's going to be about the way it's always been. Aren't you glad I shared that with you? It's not everyone who gets to hear this.*

*The tide comes in and then what? It goes back out. It's been that way for at least 6,000 years of recorded history.*

*It gets light and then what? It turns dark.*

*The next season after fall is - ? Winter, of course. Every time, without fail, for at least 6,000 years. It isn't going to change.*

*Six thousand years of recorded history reads like this: opportunity mixed with difficulty. It isn't going to change. "So," you ask, "how will my life change?" When you change!*

# THE PROCESS OF CHANGE
### (an excerpt from "The Five Major Pieces to the Life Puzzle")

*Change comes from one of two sources. First, we may be driven to change out of desperation. Sometimes our circumstances can become so out-of-control that we almost abandon our search for answers because our lives seem to be filled only with irresolvable questions. But it is this overwhelming sense of desperation that finally drives us to look for the solutions. Desperation is the final and inevitable result of months or years of accumulated neglect that brings us to that point in time where we find ourselves driven by urgent necessity to find immediate answers to life's accumulated challenges.*

*The second source that drives us to make changes in our lives is inspiration. Hopefully, that is where you find yourself right now - about to become sufficiently inspired to make major and dramatic changes in your life.*

# THE SPRING
## (an excerpt from "The Seasons of Life")

*Following the turbulence of winter comes the season of activity and opportunity called spring. It is the season for entering the fertile fields of life with seed, knowledge, commitment, and a determined effort. It is not a time to linger, nor to ponder the possibilities of failure. Foolish is the one who would allow springtime to pass while dwelling upon the memory of the successful crop last fall or the failure to reap last fall in spite of the massive efforts of last spring.*

*It is a natural characteristic of springtime to present itself ever so briefly or to lull us into inactivity with its bounteous beauty. Do not pause too long to soak in the aroma of the blossoming flowers, lest you awaken to find springtime gone, with your seed still in your sack.*

# NITTY-GRITTY REASONS
(an excerpt from "Seven Strategies
for Wealth and Happiness")

*Wouldn't it be wonderful to be motivated to achievement by such a lofty goal as benevolence? I must confess, however, that in the early years of my struggle to succeed my motivation was a lot more down-to-earth. My reason for succeeding was more basic. In fact, it fell into the category of what I like to call "nitty-gritty reasons." A nitty-gritty reason is the kind that any one of us can have - at any time, on any day - and it can cause our lives to change. Let me tell you what happened to me.*

*Shortly before I met Mr. Shoaff I was lounging at home one day when I heard a knock at the door. It was a timid, hesitant knock. When I opened the door I looked down to see a pair of big brown eyes staring up at me. There stood a frail little girl of about ten. She told me, with all the courage and determination her little heart could muster, that she was selling Girl Scout cookies. It was a masterful presentation - several flavors, a special deal, and only two dollars per box. How could anyone refuse? Finally, with a big smile and ever-so-politely, she asked me to buy.*

*And I wanted to. Oh, how I wanted to!*

*Except for one thing. I didn't have two dollars! Boy, was I embarrassed! Here I was - a father, had been to college, was gainfully employed - and yet I didn't have two dollars to my name.*

*Naturally, I couldn't tell this to the little girl with the big, brown eyes. So I did the next best thing. I lied to her. I said, "Thanks, but I've already bought Girl Scout cookies this year. And I've still got plenty in the house."*

*Now that simply wasn't true. But it was the only thing I could think of to get me off the hook. And it did. The little girl said, "That's okay, sir. Thank you very much." And with that, she turned around and went on her way.*

*I stared after her for what seemed like a very long time. Finally, I closed the door behind me and, leaning my back to it, cried out, "I don't want to live like this anymore. I've had it with being broke, and I've had it with lying. I'll never be embarrassed again by not having any money in my pocket."*

*That was the day I promised myself to earn enough money to always have several hundred dollars in my pocket at all times.*

# HCI's Business Self-Help Books

## What You Want, Wants You
How to Get Out of Your Rut
*Debra Jones*

People in the 1990s are reevaluating their lifestyles as never before. With the stability of tenured positions in large corporations becoming a thing of the past, many workers are rethinking their career choices to be more in tune with what they really want to do. Here Debra Jones, marketing whiz extraordinaire, gives you a game plan for digging yourself out of the quagmire of indecision and hopelessness in order to find your life path. An inspiring book that will leave you revitalized.
Code 3677 ..............................$9.95

## Networking Success
How to Turn Business & Financial Relationships into Fun & Profit
*Anne Boe*

How to Turn Business & Financial Relationships into Fun & Profit
Anne Boe
Author of *Is Your Net-Working?*

Networking is the business tool of the 1990s—(a must for keeping the competitive edge that separates the successful from the unsuccessful. Along with networking's unquestioned value in business, it's also useful in personal relationships. Here master networker Anne Boe describes ideas for developing, nurturing and growing your relationships, financial contacts and career networks for peak performance on and off the job.
Code 3650 .........................................$12.95

## How to Get What You Want from Almost Anyone
Your Self-Defense Consumer Guide
*T. Scott Gross*

The author gives his secrets for dealing with everyone from waiters, salesclerks and service attendants, to car salesmen and real estate agents. With an emphasis on the importance of being a good customer and having fun without being taken, T. Scott Gross explains: why you must know—and expect—what you want; what the proven strategies for getting good service are; how to effectively complain about and *correct* poor service; and how to get the best deal (or steal) possible.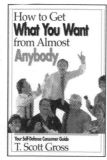
Code 3715 ............................$10.95

Available at your favorite bookstore or call 1-800-441-5569 for Visa or MasterCard orders. Prices do not include shipping and handling.
Your response code is **HCI.**

# Motivate and Inspire

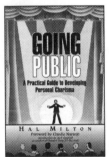